Fireheart

Collection Two

Winter

ISBN-13: 9798376214152

Cover design by: Amazon Stock/Winter Gray
Printed by Amazon Kindle Direct Publishing.

To a community who gave me support when the world was imploding, even though I don't see or speak to any of you nearly enough anymore.

To loves past, present, and future.

To family and those lost before I could say goodbye.

To you.

Thank you.

Introduction

First off, I must admit that the poems that are on these pages have been written for a while already. I was in the middle of editing and proofing You Beautiful Monster and the itch to keep going was fresh. And I had almost all of these written, and then... Covid. The pandemic started, and everything outright went to shit in my world (and everywhere else.)

So it got shelved. But not.. openly.
I kept saying to others (and myself) that "I just need to edit it. Once it's edited, I'll put it out as well."
And I kept saying that for... three years?

Mostly I stalled and hesitated because I was scared.
Scared to put more words out there.
Scared to have people read them after the first book, and see nothing new.
Scared to.. not have grown.
And that's partly still true.
At the time, these were the same words; they weren't indicative of any growth. I had started editing, and then stopped.

The document with everything in it hadn't been touched since April of '22 before today (1/18/23, for those keeping track; again, I'm sorry!) and even between now and then so *so* much has changed.

But... here we are. Because even if I'm going to hold off and hesitate, I'm a man of my word. And I told you that I would do a second one of these. And in being true to you and to myself, I haven't removed any of the words I wrote when my brain was still in the mindset that created the first collection, even if it has well and truly changed in the time since.

I do still write. I'm actually working on a story. (Here's a teaser: It's dirty, because.. well, it's me we're talking about here.)

And I am still writing poems, although less sad boy shite and more... finding light in the wind-shifted branches of shade trees, love in the hearts of strangers, and pleasant safety in the unknowable freedom of hope.

Read these words from the time before, and please never forget that growth isn't linear, time isn't cruel, and happiness isn't waiting in the hands of any other person.

I love you.
Always and forever.

-Winter

- Turning Point -

Fix the world.
These dark days cannot be all that's left.

We're better than our worst parts.

No matter
the other people
in my world
or my life.

I will always hold a place
in my heart
for you.

- Terminal -

"Distance makes the heart grow fonder."
She said to me as she went,
planes boarding in the background.

A hug
A kiss
And ache as the crowd blended her into their
form.

Distance is agony.
Time waits for no man.

Help me wind the clock back.

A thousand things I could say,
"It'll be okay."
"It gets easier to do."
"I'm here for you."

All feel too generic,
almost condescending to your pain
despite being exactly what I needed to hear
when I was in your shoes;
I didn't want to hear it.
It felt too fake; too much.
But at the same time, not enough.

I can't take it away.
I can't ease the struggle with my hands.
I can only hold you,
be a sturdy place to rest your soul,
until your roots being to take hold
and you grow once more.

And I am so very sorry.

- Traveling -

I want to see a million sights.
Cityscapes aglow with vibrant light.

I wanted to see them with you.

The constant feeling of something new.
Looking across a skyline,
I reach to wrap your hand in mine.
I absently find empty air.

…Of course
you're not there.

Why would you be?

"You can never own me."

I'm not trying to;
I just wanted to feel loved;
Entirely different things.
And now I'm sitting here
in this darkened room,
falling out of my own head
at a thousand miles an hour.

Dropping from the emotional atmosphere
with your words like
pinholes
in my parachute.

Praying to not feel alone.

- Proverbial Bullshit #1 -

They say "It's not what you know, but who."
But I am a culmination of what I know.

They say "Two wrongs don't make a right."
No, but they'll make you downright depressed.

They say, "The pen is mightier than the sword."
But I believe they can both cut equally as deep.

They say "Hope for the best, but prepare for the worst."
And honestly?
That one's sound advice.

Doubt is a powerful adversary;

It will grab you by the shoulders,
drag you through the mud,
slam your face into every wall.

It will beat you down
and not give you a single moment
to breathe.

Fight it.
Tooth and nail.

- Future Tense -

It is real.
It is coming.
It is inevitable,
and daunting.
It will be awful,
and awe filled.
Terrifying,
and terrific.

But it will happen.
Whether you're
ready or not.

Here it comes.

It took a *lifetime* to realize what you meant to me.

But only a *moment* to ensure you never knew.

- Crashing Down -

"It's beautiful," she said.

The massive waterfall ever rushing downward in front of us, mist overtaking everything in sight.

"This strange visual of water falling so in love with gravity that it completely gives up control."

She turned to me,
a suddenly sad look in her eyes,
"Or is it gravity?
Taking advantage,
pulling water, hell… everything,
down against its will?"

And for a moment,
I couldn't answer.

I was too busy
relating to this beauty of physics.

I wake up sad these days.
A weight resting on my chest, pressure I can't
categorize and an overbearing *feeling* that nothing I
do is right.

- Grieve -

A cavalcade of emotions;
my thoughts in a grim procession throughout my
mind.

The funeral of self-confidence.

It was killed by anxiety,
brutally and without remorse and hesitation.

I didn't even get to say goodbye.

Laid out upon the table
Depictions of potency:
Past
Present
Future
Conflicts and resolutions.

Answers to questions I can't begin to ask aloud.

- Shipwreck -

I woke t'find myself
adrift upon dark waters.
The air all 'round hazy and thick.
Unsure of how I found myself here,
unaware of where here even was.
Suddenly a faint flicker a'light,
cast out from the mire ahead.
Far, yet constant;
A lighthouse t'guide me home.

A growing unease swell'd within me,
as a rushing static of sound began to overtake.

Sinking
Spiraling
Drowning in worry
Reaching for someone
Anyone
I found you
But
We were both struggling
So I pushed
And dug my feet in
Gave you a foundation

(One of us needed to survive the flood)

- It's Complicated -

What we do for each other,
What we look for in others,
How we support and care for each other.

A complex partnership of
loose bindings and balanced emotions,
akin to precarious building blocks
held together with rubber bands;

We are flexible but supportive.

But when anyone asks?
Well…

I see you.

And your happiness.

And I miss being part of it.

Help me forget all my worries;
intertwine your fingers in mine,
your lips,
your soul,
lose each other in our reckless chaos.

Not because it's all we have;
it isn't.

But rather because it is a power,
something we can control
in this world of things
that move without us;
In spite of us.

The world spins regardless,
but in these moments
it doesn't matter.

- Okay -

Can't let myself break.
Can't give in to my sadness.
Can't let the cracks show.

I don't have the luxury to allow
myself to be anything less than

Okay.

But my soul is tearing
a hole in my façade.

It's screaming for help.
I just want to be…

You shouldn't only feel comfortable wearing
things that divert attention instead of attract it;
Your armor doesn't have to be camouflage;
it can be elegant,
beautiful,
well-thought out
shades of intensity and ferocity.

Besides, it not called
"dressed to kill"
for nothing.

- Rewind -

I am a burned bridge.
A closed door;
A turned page.

Do you want to go back to before (as bad as I
do?)

I'm scared to say what I'm thinking.

That I'm just here to fill a void;
A placeholder to satisfy
needs and cravings
loneliness
until you get what you truly want.

Because I know for a fact it isn't me.
And when you get it?
What will I do?

- Siren's Song -

Rest yourself against my shores;
Worry not for the sharpness of stones.

The tide will bring you back to me;
The depths will sleep your bones.

Come bask upon these ivory sands;
Let nature pick you clean.

You'll not feel the heart ripped from your chest;
The melody holds you like a dream.

Everyone has a vice.
Be it
the drink
the drug
the thrill of something taboo
or otherwise immoral.

Everyone has a vice.
But why…

why are you mine?

One last flicker of flame
the embers of a lost love
smoldering among the ashes
of a fire that was left unkindled.

One last time,
dance this waltz;

Our arson of the heart.

This one will make you feel
uncomfortable because I know you know
when I'm talking about her;

Describing details,
nuances,
the feel of her lips,
the ache in my hands,
knowing full well that my words
can and do evoke emotions or even..
discomfort.

I
don't
write
them
for
you.

- Day I -

I have written testaments of
The fire and fury you carry within yourself
I will continue do so until
I am consumed

And upon that day I will die gladly
Having chronicled

The love within you.

Someday I shall overcome
This festered wound I've held
Yet unhealed by time or care

A malady of the heart
Shattered in my chest
Slicing up my insides
Bleeding injuries I try not to share.

I cannot bury it
I cannot keep it
Time doesn't heal all wounds
And this is mine alone to bear.

- Day 3 -

What do I have to offer?
What price have I yet to pay?
What sins are left to ask of me?
I cannot absolve myself away.

Be it the gallows
Or the guillotine?
A pyre or firing squad?
Death does not yet beseech me;
You will not place me beneath the sod.

Penance I do not require.
I made the choices that now stand.
Weights rest upon my heart

And cold irons upon my hands.

- Day 4 -

Resolve comes at a heavy price
It constantly is fought
By longing
Desire
Willingness
To just give in.

Resist.
Those voices will quiet.

Eventually.

I don't have it in me
To make myself move
To make myself "better"
Or even care why.
I could however
Dress
Clean up
And find the energy
To start walking

And simply

Never

Stop

I can't burn it away
Despite the fire

I can't wash it away
Despite the rain

This coming storm rests upon my heart
And this calamity wrought with pain.

It's the things you do so easily with him
That you never wanted from me
It's the things you smile about
That never got the same response
When it was mine
It's the things you let him do
That no one else could have ever
Gotten away with

He's even taken my words.
Why does that hurt the worst?

Missed chances
Lost to time
You can't get them back

You can only proceed
One foot
In front
Of the other.

Extrovert in isolation
Climbing the walls
Bound in a cage of my own design
Scrambling to retain a semblance of sanity

Sisyphus would be jealous
Hades would be proud

- Day 10 -

I could stay in this room all day
Isolating ever further
Holding myself hostage
And not see you even once.

It wouldn't be much different
Than it has been for the past few days.
Even though I've seen you
It barely feels like you're here.

You're tired of me.
I'm tired of me.

So I guess I'll remove myself.

Something feels
Wrong
Out of place
Disjointed and disconnected
Disconcerting
In the air
In me

I can't place me it

- Day 12 -

I feel like
I'm losing steam
Spinning my wheels
Sputtering so close to the finish
Making my best attempt
But traction is failing
And I'm
Stuck.

- Day 13 -

The thirteenth hour
Of my thirtieth year
I was sitting absently
At a fountain in Atlanta
Contemplating the end
And what I would do
To bring it about.
The word "no." etched
Into my wrist
Staring back at me in indignation
At my thoughts.
Beckoning me to overcome
Overrule
Jump the hurdle
Continue the race.

Fate saw fit to intervene.
Placing people in my path
Hands to reach down
Pull me to my feet
Clean my wounds
Clear my head
And give me the push
To continue.

- Day 14 -

Fuck.

I'm supposed to keep this up, I guess.
Maintain this momentum and all I can think
about is how I really don't want to.

I just want to put this down and not bother but I
know I need to keep going.

I need to form the habit.
It worked for her.
It'll work for me.

- Day 15 -

Cotton and hemp
Binding
Twisting
Intention
Aligning
Containing
Therapy
Comfort
Missing

Stand for change
Not for normalcy.

You can miss normal and want for better.
But normal doesn't miss you and did not stand for
you.

- Day 17 -

Butterflies
Happy feelings
Anxious thoughts
What happens next?

Quarantine is the worst time
To learn how someone feels

(It has to end soon. Right?)

Once again I seek to feel
Skin under my hands
Pulse against pulse
Faltering breaths
Heat that cannot be mimicked

A fire that burns deeply
A passion that lights the darkness

Lustful comfort on a cold night

- Day 19 -

It seems so simple
"The heart wants what it wants"

And yet
In the moments after
Does everyone else think
(In whatever context)

"This is what I deserve."

The other day
I was asked

"If I die are you gonna care?"

And it shook me to my core.

Of course I would.
Just the notion I might not
Made me question everything.
I shook myself out of it today.

And now I'm almost scared
To ask if you're still here.

Am I so aversive
That in your sleep
You choose to berate me?

Does that person
In your subconscious
Express how you truly feel?

I'm sure it isn't
But gods, that person
Treats me the worst

I hate this feeling the worst.
That I'm not only not good enough to matter.
But that I know I shouldn't invest so much.

Other people do not do this towards me.
Why should I to them?
Why should I care?
Why do I fucking care?
Why am I feelings and why do I need them?

Do I?
Truly?

- Day 23 -

I thought I was getting better

Turns out I was just getting used to it
Maybe tomorrow will be better
But it's likely I'll just be acclimated
Again.

I need relief.
Comfort I cannot find.
Sanity I cannot hold.
I am scared.

- Day 24 -

Tender intimacy
Genuine honesty
Compatibility
I never thought to find.

Worth the wait;
Worth the distance;
Worth the past.

A decade in the making.

- Day 25 -

The gods have a sense of humor.
They've given me what I never thought.

It holds so many aspects
I was unprepared for.

And yet, I find myself eager.

How did I get here?

- Day 26 -

Gloomy Sunday
Uneasy minds

A monotonous task seems overwhelming.

Give me strength.

Pour me another
Cup of well-intended misery
Sadness with a splash of regret
And a single ice cube
To cut the burn with cold.

Wisps of smoke
Embers of enlightenment
Hazy futures clouded
By the unfortunate past
Somewhere there is an end

Is it in sight?
Just around the next sunrise?

Or miles away
Patient for the eventual arrival?

I will not go out so easily.

I've lost my words again.

Not for lack of trying
Or having proper motivation.

It just seems as though
A landslide came through
And derailed
My train of thought

Distance is a funny thing:

Sometimes you need it;
Other times you can't stand it.
It can be physical
Emotional
Chronological
But it brings change
And that is welcomed
With tender anticipation.

I am the equivocation of
mindless rambling
hopeless romanticism
heartsick longing
numbing depression
ambivalent confidence
callous self-loathing
and flagrant
(almost flippant)
 optimism.

 I hate myself sometimes;
I wouldn't want to be anyone else at others.

 It makes clear to me my current situation.

When I'm ready.
I'll never be that person to you.
You deserve love and happiness.
I just keep making bad decisions.
You're so sweet.
And kind.
You're a better person.
Why did I want you?
What were you thinking?
You're freaking out.
It was just what came first, sorry.
But you're really nice.

(Words I've heard over the years.)

A glimpse
A flashing memory of

Was it a better time?
Or was it just the best we had
While we were searching
For what we really wanted?
Is it bad that I'd go back in time
To see if I could change the present?

Nostalgia is such a fickle mistress.

Deadlines
Dead conversations
Moments lost in the flow of
Time

Upstream against the current
Fighting inevitability
It never feels like there's enough

Going

Going

Gone but never stopping
To smell the flowers
Or feel the breeze

It's all swept away

I dreamt of you
Curled against me
Sleeping peacefully
Stirring gently as I bent my neck
To kiss the crown of your head
Resting upon my chest
Your arm wrapped across my waist
Tightened but for a moment
A contented sound
Slipping from your lips

It was quite a dream, wasn't it.

All these years I miss it still.

What is so unreal about
Expressing oneself?

Creativity is exposure,
The soul unwrapped;
Un-warped by the lens of fitting in.

Deepest loves
Darkest fears
Brought to the light
In words or colors

Paint a picture however you wish
But paint it straight from your soul.

I try not to weary of
Perhaps and maybe
Soft no's
From hesitant hearts
Meant with earnest intent.

What's left of myself
To work on
To remake
Until I find what I'm missing

What I'm looking for.

She sat, calmly at the table, speaking slowly,

"Break me down,
Bend my knee;
Cast a fire into my soul,
And bleed the devil into me.
Take the lust and breathe the sin,
Soak my heart in your fuel
And set alight every desire
I have but this body to give;
I have but these hands to wield;
But they are yours
Should you earn them."

And for a moment,
I wondered who was in control.

Nestled
Firmly within our form
Contained inside the cages we carry
Locked by design
Yet those we think worthy
Reach easily between the bars.

Our songbirds flutter at their grasp
Uncertain of the melody

Our coal miners' canaries try to warn us
Frantic before the poisonous shade

Our crows call out in memory
Of past sweetness in sublime savagery

An aviary of good intentions

Our metaphorical menagerie

It is only in the shattering when we find ourselves.

Broken in the hands of one who will not recover
all the pieces.

I will bind my hands in irons
Chains and ropes
To illicit the feeling
Of being held in someone's grasp

Does that speak to loneliness
Or perversion

Malaise
Or maliciousness

Place your hands upon
Hold down until the animal breaks free
Fight to overtake control
Lose beautifully

(You're winning this dangerous game)

Forty-one hundred Fifty-four miles.

Between where I am,
And where I want to be.

An ocean and a pandemic
Are all that keep me from you.

The hitch in your breath
The little gasp as I find you

Gravity takes me and I fall
A molten protector for you

Inspiration comes in waves
Like ice cream sick on a summer Sunday
The endorphins rush
Creativity climbs from the core
Tracing itself out through my fingertips
And suddenly the feelings rush over me
I find myself criticizing my shore

Looking for answers
Of questions unasked
Finding the imposter syndrome
Just underneath the water's edge

Is all I am my kindness?
Once you break the surface and sink in
Is all that's left are shipwrecks
Reminders of the past preserved in memory
Instead of worn and weathered
By the winds of time.

Is that why
I can't get over you?

Recollections of
Sunset skies and bright embers
Calloused memories
An inner struggle

Who is left for me to be
Expressing myself
Lost cacophony
Momentary bewildered
By crushing silence

I am so touch-starved
That this bed feels like a desert
Expansive and barren
So isolated
That I wonder who would hear me scream
In this microcosm of my life
So heartsick
That I almost forget the feeling because
Anything different feels foreign
So lost
Among the echoes of the lives I've lived

That currently I don't know myself

A refreshing drink
on a summer day.

The warmth of a fire
during the first snow.

Three words that have the power
to move mountains;
to carve channels;
to take flight.

This year has been
Testing.

Things started well, only to
Crumble.

And every little light
Fading.

I'm losing it all to time
Passing.

Every time I close my eyes:

Frantically roaming hands.
Heated, labored breathing.

Fervent, lustful clashing of needs, mouths, and bodies.

Aching for,
Begging for,
Unhindered, primal release.

Maybe this is why I can't sleep;

Why my body aches for even the most simplistic
of human contact.

These days it always feels like
I'm
Too little *too* late
Too old
Too out of touch
Too close
Too distant
Last off the line
Last to realize

Last to understand that things move on
That people move on
That you *have* to move on
It's been three years, you should move on
It's been *so* many faces ago, you should move on
It's been a lifetime, you should *move on*
She doesn't *love you* anymore, you..

But instead you write about it.
You pine for things you don't get to have anymore
because you threw it all away.
Over what?

Over nothing more than a moment where you felt
betrayed
so you
betrayed yourself
and more importantly
you betrayed *her*
And now all that's left is a friendship nestled in
the ashes of a love that *you didn't deserve* in the first
place.

But you tasted it,
for *years* that felt like *seconds*.

You became addicted to the drug
that danced across your lips
And like a junkie out of recovery
with a wish to overcome
You tease yourself with the thought
that you can exist around it;
That it won't control you;
That it won't consume you.

Who are *you?*
Who do you *think you* are?

Who gave you the right to think your story
matters?
That you're not just another name in her story
A supporting role
That's waiting to be recast
Because she needed your support
And you..

You forgot *all* of your lines.

What is this feeling?

Falling?
Why?

Is it because
I'm finally finding comfort and relaxation?

Or has the ground been ripped from underneath
me and I just haven't noticed yet?

It's the little things:

The good morning messages
The comforting smile
Existing in this space with you

These things remind me of why
I am alive.

I would miss them too much otherwise.

Let this last forever.
Let these dreams remain lucid in my mind.

This vision of the world I want,
the life I've glimpsed;
grasped at with imaginary fingers.

It isn't perfect;
honestly it's rather disheveled.
But it's with you,
And that is all I need.

Today is a day of
painted hearts.
Apprehensive conversations,
embellished in a distance
that feels much farther than
normal.

Familiar pains that
reawaken
icy reminders

of swearing things would
never
be this way again.

I miss when the world was simpler.

I miss when I didn't feel so defeated.

I miss the feeling of.. feeling.

I miss you, my one.

It is all around me.
Echoes in the wind.
Brushing across my skin.
Every catch in my chest when I close my eyes
and amidst every night of sleepless unrest.

I have forgotten my own happiness in wishing for
yours.

All I have are faint reminders.

Am I back too early?
Was I gone too long?

Have I missed any opportunity
to reclaim this portion of my life?
Do I throw in the towel?

- Legal Drug -

Caffeine (for all that it is) is a slow poison.
Or rather, it causes the slowest poison I have
knowledge of.
It cracks open - ever so slightly - the dam that
holds back the lake of anxiety,
clenched jaws, and overthinking
that I have worked myself ragged to contain.

The trickling toxins flow back into my stream of
thoughts
and gradually the ecosystem is tainted
and I am once again fighting to contain the spread
before it contaminates the geography around it.

But it always leaches into the soil. Or rather, soul.

I notice it first in my conversations.
In my doubting the intent of the people
whom I normally trust implicitly.
It rides their words like a scent in the wind,
and betrays their nonexistent thoughts towards me
so that all I can do is feel
unworthy
of their friendship.

- Do you Remember? -

Do you remember the first time you fell truly in love?

Not the innocent childlike love of youth,
but the first time that you
looked at someone and knew
that you would give them anything;
that you would give up anything for their world?
Just for them to stay a part of yours?

Do you remember the first time you lost your love?

The first time that all you could do
to keep from losing yourself was to
steel yourself in your grief,
and take every step as though the earth was
falling away behind you?
Falling into the pit in your stomach
and the nothingness wrapping around you,
clinging to every memory?

Do you remember the first true regret you ever had?

The first honest mistake that you will never be
able to take back?
And seeing every action past that point ripple
outwards like a wave
from a stone cast into still water?
Knowing that every moment from then on would
be irrevocably different,
and all you could do was
wish that the stone were never cast?

I lie awake at night with these thoughts.

They scream their baleful echoes
when the world is silent and still.
They betray themselves
behind my eyes and
in the tone of my voice.
At times I would give anything to lose them.
Others I would give anything to keep.
But they are mine.
And I am yours.

Even though I may never be.

I ask not for your forever,
For a future we cannot know.

I ask not for your loyalty,
Because no love is set in stone.

I ask not for your forgiveness,
For a past I cannot change.

I ask not for your happiness,
In hopes to offset any pain.

I only wish from you these things,
And will deliver such in return:

Intelligence when I mistake myself;
Love when I do not love myself;
Compassion when I lose myself;
Honesty when I do not know.

I don't care about the past
the future
or my place in it.

I care about here
and now
and the closeness between us.

- Fireheart -

Grace in embers.
Fury in a blaze.

Heat and light
So violently powerful
It vaporizes the very tears
From each and every anguish.

It cannot be quenched.

It
Will
Not
Be
Quenched.

Only tended. And fed.

Eventually
I'll be able to be okay
I'll be able to disconnect
and see and hear the things
that right now make me feel
unwanted,
unneeded,
and unnecessary.

Eventually I'll get over my feelings.
Eventually I'll make my heart listen to me.
Eventually.

I just miss the feeling
of what I thought was love.
That warmth
that wasn't fiery passion,
but rather a gentle glow
radiating from my chest
like I'd swallowed a dozen fireflies.

The change in atmosphere
that came with her fingers in my hair,
my name upon her lips,
the shine in her smiling eyes.

Anyone can see how I was mistaken.

You used my true name.
Held it aloft
among your words
when you wanted my embrace

And I followed it.
That sacred piece of me
that I don't let everyone use.

And you led me
into comfort
into your bed
with those few letters.

A name has power.
And you know mine.

Was that a mistake?

A chemical to balance
Emotions and expressiveness
Like perfect scales
Imperfections can be costly
When emotions weigh heavy as lead
And you're paying pennies for charcoal

Penny for your thoughts
Pound for your pleasures
Bankrupting your savings

For blissful equilibrium
A steady moment upon
The seas of uncertainty
Salvation for a castaway
Flying high
Getting higher

Are you high enough
To fight the gravity
Of your mind?

Maybe someday
I will understand
What it means
To be loved unconditionally

(But not today.)

It's time.
There is no way back;
Only moving forward.
Upon your own two feet.

No handrails, no safety net.

Be scared.
Be brave.

Take the leap.

I'm not asking anyone
to hold my life together;
To use their time or energy to
glue my edges
and press tightly until I'm fine.

I can do that on my own.
I'm just begging for the comfort
of a trusted person's embrace.
Because the world is cold enough;

Do we have to be to each other?

"Only you can truly make yourself happy."

...Not according to the sounds
　　　　that hung in the air last night.

- Will you miss me? -

I do not want for you out of love
Or lust
Or unintended emotion.

I want for you because at one time
You held me in your arms and told me that you
loved me. And in that moment
I couldn't recall a time I felt less alone.

But that's all over now.
Now I sit in these cold dark rooms
And anxiously agonize over what I can't begin to
understand.

What did I do?
What did I say to make you turn away and take
that liberating feeling of welcomeness and warmth
with you?
What could I have done differently?

The answer is evident.
Nothing.

The heart wants what it wants and there is no force on earth or in the heavens that can make it deviate from that.
And you? You just didn't want me.
But instead of discarding me like the toy you've outgrown; instead you hold me at arm's length and remind me I'm on my own.

You remind me that I can hold you but I cannot have you.
And what is holding you worth if you only want the embrace of anyone who isn't me?

What is holding you worth if all you are to me is what I see?

When I look inside the mirror and see the life I used to know?

What life can I build with you if in the end I am still alone?

What is it worth to wake up knowing that someday I will not wake up with your light in my life?

And like a mosquito light.
I am hopelessly enraptured in the thing that I
should not want.
Drawn to the inexorable conclusion of my short
lived saga.
A drop in the bucket of history that will not miss
me.

Will you miss me?

Sometimes I feel
That the only way I can survive
Is to lock my heart away
Pretend it doesn't exist

So I can be whatever
To whoever
Without my own wants
To get in the way.

It's ironic.

Resolve things.
We're taught that at a young age.

"Clean your plate before you can have dessert"
"Pick up your toys when you're done playing"

So why is that so hard for us?
We add more people to our lives,
More issues,
More complications,
Without resolving anything we've already begun.

We learned nothing.

I am broken down.
Like a car on the side of the road
That can't seem to start.
My check engine light is on
And I don't have any idea why.

Did I push too hard?
Have I ran too many miles?

I need a mechanic.
I need help.

Bite down on your thumb.
Chew your lip until you bleed.
Accept the fact that your shell
Isn't permanent or invincible.

And not everyone else enjoys it.
Sometimes not even you yourself.
But someone out there does.
Someone sees past it.
To the potential that is within.

There is a chill in the air.
Not from the weather
Or the season

But from a lack of you.

Someone.
Anyone.

Is it going to be okay?
Am I going to be okay?

'You can feel it coming. Again.'

...Stop.

'The separation. The loss of someone you hold dear.'

...No.

'It's on the top of their tongue. They can't bear you anymore. They didn't sign up for your kind of crazy.'

...maybe you're right. But I'd hope to know beforehand.

'...What makes you think you don't?'

Have you ever watched someone fall?
Either willingly taking the leap
or swept off their feet
before they realized what was happening?

How sometimes they
close their eyes
accept their fate
or struggle and fight
all the way
down?

Ever watch someone you care about
fall in love without you?

I need to sever this link;
This empathic connection
that makes me experience
everything
that those closest to me feel by proxy.

I am envious of the ones
who make you feel this happy.

I am envious that
I can't find this happiness in my own existence.

I can't always fit your wants and needs.
It's just.. not within my ability.

But I can hope you want me for more than just
what I can give you.

I hope I am myself worth being around.

Grasping
For contact
For the faintest connection
The clearest signal between two entities

Casting emotion and intention
Clearing the airwaves
Communicating in the silence

Quiet my brain with interlaced fingers
Quiet my soul
With wordless sincerity

These words are formed
From the depths of my heart
They slide from my soul
Out through my fingertips

Dripping
Dark and tainted
Imbalanced humours
Only to be bled
Delicately with surgical precision
Intricate sorrows across canvas

Like a scalpel in deft hands

What changed
To make you move beyond
What about me
Made you decide
I wasn't worth it.

Now you fill that space
With anything that isn't me
And I'm left wondering if
I'll ever feel your warmth again.

Are you afraid I'll change
Ask for more than you think I should
I've already crossed that bridge
And won't turn back

But we both have needs
And I still enjoy yours

You gave me a space in your heart
Amongst the people you cherish
You held me, claimed me
Entwined your existence with mine.

But those strings have frayed
And now
Between us
There's a space in your heart.

Tonight
Amidst the chill and weather
Use my body as the kindling
Stoke the flames of passion
Burn away the chill
Warm yourself

It's the best use for me.

When do you realize
The change in the air
The Difference
In behavior

The nights becoming
A little less colder
A little less Lonely

When does it pass your mind
That you're actually
Loved

I will always love
"Too much"
for some people.

If that's a curse,
then I feel sorry for you.

My fingers ache to
trace the curves;
The rises and falls,
and feel the faintest spark
of your need
of my touch.

I'm so tired.
So angry.
So ready to just give in.
Mostly, I'm just so afraid this is
how things are meant to be.

(I can't even take solace in commiserating arms.)

- Locked -

There are rooms;
Places inside my heart I will not enter.

Inside their walls
All of the parts of my past
Of my loves
That I dare not think about.

Unfortunately
The key to every door
Held by every person
Their name engraved
And a small fire
Burning yet
untended.

I could not evict them.

I am told to
Make space for myself
Let the past go
Worry not for them
And yet I cannot.

I can't find the keys.

Enrapture me in your elegance.
Envelop me in your sin.
Convey my soul to
whatever may await us,
and bury my bones
in the garden
of your memories,
so that your future growth
will be bolstered
by the nourishment of my sacrifice.

But let my time remaining
be spent enthralled in the feelings
of how your body feels by mine,
and how my mind calms
when your heartbeat resonates through my temple.

(No one can say I'm not devout.)

I've been so many things
A friend, a lover
A secret, a caretaker
Even once or twice
A cruel heartbreaker

But that's all in the past.
Now... now I'm just me.

(Whatever I'm needed to be.
What do you want me to be?)

- Midnight Mass -

I miss the pleasurable things tonight.
Hands on skin,
Caressing and teasing.
Fingers intertwined,
Breathing intermingled.
Entering the places that are
Truly
Deviously
Sacred.

A chorus of desire,
A procession of purest sin.

Like the tide
you drift in and out of my life.

Like the tide,
I would be forever changed by a lack of you.

Nature is violent
Unforgiving
Unconcerned with you
It disregards you
As we have disregarded it
Mistreated
Damaged
Not in a sudden upheaval
But in a slow
Yet equally deliberate
Devastation.

Sticks in place
Stones arranged
Bones of nature
Words in embers

"Break and crackle,
Burned to ash."

I crossed paths with a stranger.
No words were exchanged;
Simple cursory glances.

In that heartbeat I saw
Our entire future together;
Highs and lows,
Love and sadness.

To be continued.

Made in the USA
Columbia, SC
06 August 2023

bb1ed252-23bc-4a2f-a47f-4e5fdaceac45R01